D0105371

TOO SMART
TO BE RICH

ON BEING A YUFFIE

This book balances the scale on the mislabeled "yuppie" generation. It is a declaration of the revolution of moderate and moderating expectations.

Eugene J. McCarthy
Former U. S. Senator

TOO SMART
TO BE RICH

ON BEING A YUFFIE

PATTY FRIEDMANN

NEW CHAPTER PRESS, NEW YORK

Permission to quote from the following is gratefully acknowledged.

A Thousand Clowns by Herb Gardner. Copyright © 1961, 1962 by Herb Gardner
and Irwin A. Cantor, trustee. Published in New York by Random House, Inc., and
simultaneously in Toronto, Canada, by Random House of Canada, Limited. Used
by permission of author.

How to Be a Jewish Mother by Dan Greenburg. Copyright © 1964, 1965 by Dan
Greenburg. Published by Price/Stern/Sloan, Los Angeles. Used by permission of
author.

The lines from "nobody loses all the time" from IS 5 by E. E. Cummings are used
by permission of Liveright Publishing Corporation. Copyright © 1985 by E. E.
Cummings Trust. Copyright 1926 by Horace Liveright. Copyright 1954 by E. E.
Cummings. Copyright 1985 by George James Firmage.

Book design by Kathleen Joffrion
Illustrations by Bunny Matthews
Cover design by Barbara Marks/Lynne Kopcik

Printed in the United States of America

165/95

DEDICATION

This book is dedicated to the memory of my father, Werner Friedmann. In more ways than one.

ACKNOWLEDGMENTS

A humble thank you to Ken and Ellen Taylor, who allowed me to bask in their erudition until I could pass it off as mine. Thanks to Linda Hobson, who's still my last word in things literate, as well as to Betsy Petersen, who's always there with an answer. I'll always be grateful to Mike Chafetz who, without knowing me, gave me one of life's great opportunities—the chance to work with Wendy Crisp. Seriously.

To my husband, Bob Skinner, I'm deeply appreciative for his critical eye, his access to every obscure fact, and his capacity to support me in the style to which I've become accustomed.

CONTENTS

YUFFIES EVERYONE'S HEARD OF

GLOSSARY

INTRODUCTION

That's 'y' as in young, 'u' as in urban, 'f' as in failure—and 'fie' as in cute suffix for cute demographic acronym.

To paraphrase Dan Greenburg ("you don't have to be either Jewish or a mother to be a Jewish mother..."), you don't have to be young, urban, or a professional to be a yuppie. Jewish mothers, yuppies, preppies, and others who've earned whole book titles get their cachet from a state of mind. You want to be one, so you talk like one, you dress like one, maybe you go out and buy the right kind of car—that's all it takes.

Yuffies, on the other hand, are to-the-manner-born. Yuffie— young urban failure. Okay, so you don't have to be particularly young. You certainly don't have to be urban—who can afford those rents? But you do have to be a bona fide *failure*. Failure is a state of mind, you say? We'll grant you that. The yuffie feels like a flop—and the yuffie knows everybody else knows that his bank balance on the eleventh of the month is $8.47. But that's not the point. What makes the yuffie special, destiny-driven, even, is that he was on the way to becoming a yuffie on the day of his first report card. Or maybe before, when he uttered his first sentence at the age of ten months.

See, the yuffie is a failure *despite the odds*. He was born with the trappings of success. His daddy's rich, and his mama's good-looking, and his IQ is over 135. He'd probably be a yuppie if he weren't so smart. But somewhere on his life's little flow chart, where the line leads to Defining Oneself as an Adult, the yuffie bottomed out. He's living in a big-bucks-count society, and he is a dismal financial flub.

But no more! The demographers are hot on the trail of the yuffie. By the next presidential election, the Democrats are going to be courting him, and the Republicans are going to be trying to squeeze him into oblivion. He's going to be important, and he's going to be damned arrogant. With good reason. The yuffie should have a Calvinistic sort of arrogance, for not just anyone can be a yuffie. A yuppie, yes. A preppie, yes. Even a Jewish mother, if you're that perverse. But if you read through these pages in your thirty-fifth year, or your fortieth year, and find that you fill the bill, be proud. You were born to be a yuffie. You were given everything you needed to be rich and successful, and you drove it into the ground with the aplomb and finesse of true genius.

PART ONE

THE
YUFFIE
MYSTIQUE

CHAPTER ONE

BORN YUFFIE

Yuffiehood is like any psychosomatic illness. You're born with a predisposition—to migraine headaches, to ulcers, to failure. All it takes is just the right environment, and you're on your way.

It's all there from birth. You can see it was coming if you just look at your baby book. And you have a well-kept baby book, because mothers of fledgling yuffies maintain better records on their little geniuses than Congress keeps on its own proceedings. And is it all true? *You'll* never know. But you did everything at half the age you were supposed to. The baby book from the Chicago Lying-in Hospital said you were supposed to roll over at five months; you did it at two months. You should have used a spoon at eleven months; you were using a fork at six months. It's all there in aqua ink, neat printing. You even got your teeth early. And potty training—potty training! You were finished learning *that* at a year. So on top of being a failure when you're grown up, you've probably got a spastic colon. The woman set you up: who could possibly be *that* brilliant?

Ah, a child of such promise…You made all "As" in grade school, without trying. But then, nobody tries in grade school. It's later on that you began fine-honing your yuffie skills.

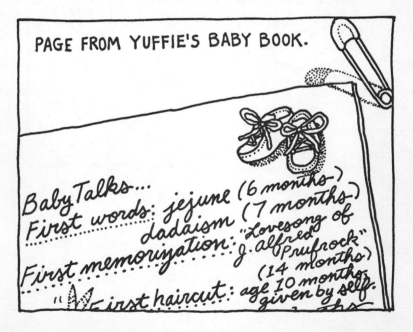

PAGE FROM YUFFIE'S BABY BOOK.

Baby Talks…
First words: jejune (6 months)
dadaism (7 months)
First memorization: "Lovesong of
J. Alfred Prufrock"
(14 months)
"…first haircut: age 10 months,
given by self.

High school, that's when the yuffie threshes himself out of the yuppie crowd. Yuffies and yuppies come from the same schools. The Westchester-Shaker Heights-Beverly Hills-Northshore Chicago public schools. The private schools. The magnet schools that parents tolerate because entrance makes a genuine show-off bauble out of their kid. Face it, in high school everyone is too gonad-oriented to spend time drawing fine lines between yuffies and yuppies. So they mingle freely. And they'll mingle freely until they read this book. In fact, it's those common origins with yuppies that ultimately keep yuffies afloat.

Threshing out. It's a matter of philosophy, truth to tell. This business of getting on the track to failure. Now parents and other oppressors probably saw the move to the failure track as an act of laziness. Or inborn rottenness. (Remember how you were a six-month-old who could spear a chunk of lambchop with a fork and grind it down fine with half a dozen molars? Your mother forgot.)

High school, yes, high school. That's where the yuffie gets his first shot at debunking everything B.F. Skinner ever stood for. Good behavior comes of rewards. The pigeon pecks the circle and gets the kernel of corn. But not the proud yuffie-to-be! In the world of A-pluses and grade point averages, the yuffie learns the first lesson in Being a Failure In a Capitalistic Society. It doesn't matter at all how smart/talented/creative a person is–what counts is the droning tedium of hard work. In high school, the ones who get the "As" aren't the ones who can write three volumes of brilliant free verse: they're the ones who memorize *Cliff's Notes* on *Julius Caesar.*

YUFFIE REPORT CARD.

Now it is perfectly acceptable for a yuffie to develop a special interest in high school. *But just one.* A yuffie can teach himself to break Pentagon codes on the computer...or speak three foreign languages, two of which are dead...or read all of Nabokov while the rest of the class is plodding through *Huckleberry Finn.* The yuffie can even get all "As" in his favorite subject, perhaps copping the Abraham Goldberg Memorial Award for Differential Calculus in the ninth grade. Just as long as the yuffie is not rewarded in a quantitative way. No cumulative 4.0s. No valedictory speeches. Valedictorians go on to Harvard undergrad and Penn Med and settle down for the rest of their lives to read x-rays or tissue slides and buy tax shelters.

Yuffies go on to Harvard, too–the SATs will undo a yuffie every time. But the yuffie majors in Folklore and Literature or

Social Relations. And the yuffie certainly is not averse to going on to graduate school—some linger there forever. (See Chapter Two.)

As for the yuffie-to-be in his youth, one more absolute rule. *The yuffie never participates in team sports.* Never. That is the training ground for corporate America. A definite yuffie no-no. It's really not even acceptable for a yuffie to have ever had a complete PE uniform all in one place at the same time. Certainly not on his body.

CHAPTER TWO

FULFILLING THE YUFFIE DESTINY

You don't need to read *Passages* to know that the years between one's 20th and 30th birthdays are years to be trashed. Throwaway years. The most golden, directed, brainless yuppie may spend the bulk of that decade in law school or med school or business school. But 95 percent of all college graduates flap around until they're 30, making mistakes which only cease to be embarrassing through long-term therapy—or the passage of time. This is especially true of the hard-core baby boomer.* You could spend the bulk of your 20s just marching around Washington hollering and smoking dope and looking up in windows and imagining that you are grand enough to be under FBI surveillance.

The road forks at age 30. The yuppies clamber off on the great search for goat cheese and BMWs. And the yuffies just keep on keeping on. Life after 30 is just an extension of the flawed questing of the 20s. It's sort of like being trapped in a time warp in your sophomore year of college, and never getting out of it.

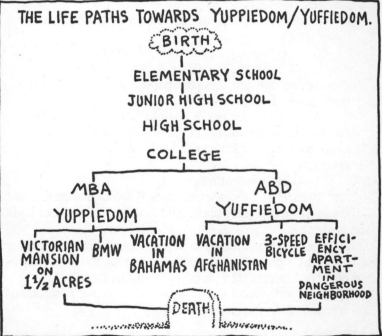

THE LIFE PATHS TOWARDS YUPPIEDOM/YUFFIEDOM.

BIRTH
ELEMENTARY SCHOOL
JUNIOR HIGH SCHOOL
HIGH SCHOOL
COLLEGE

MBA — YUPPIEDOM

ABD — YUFFIEDOM

VICTORIAN MANSION ON 1½ ACRES · BMW · VACATION IN BAHAMAS

VACATION IN AFGHANISTAN · 3-SPEED BICYCLE · EFFICIENCY APARTMENT IN DANGEROUS NEIGHBORHOOD

DEATH

Hard-core baby boomer: anyone born close enough to 1948 to have had genuine fear of the draft lottery.

What saved you from being a yuppie? You could be a fatalist, say that you were pre-programmed by the Supreme Being. You could say that you chose it of free will, but then you'd have to figure out whether that Supreme Being gave you that free will and whether He then scripted out all your free decisions.

See what we mean? Caught in the contemplative-sophomore warp for life. It's no wonder that the most far-sighted of yuffies get themselves into graduate school and hang in until their hair gets gray. "ABD"* is the most common degree on the yuffie resume.

The yuffie is a thinking person, and some very particular thoughts steered him unerringly toward failure. Where he got those thoughts is best left for his self-probing time, of which every yuffie has a great deal. (See Chapter Eleven.)

The thought process goes something like this:

"I am brilliant. Every teacher who ever gave me a C or D told my mother so in the 'if only he'd apply himself' lecture.

"I am too good to grow up to be a functionary or a paper shuffler or a peddler.

"So I won't go to medical school—doctors are well-paid technicians, like plumbers. And messy! And I won't go to law school—attorneys are paper shufflers, like petty bureaucrats. Brainless work.

"And I certainly won't go into business. Hell, my family's been coasting on great-grandpa-Irving-the-diamond-merchant's bucks since 1900. What an embarrassment.

"I will be free-floating genius."

And that's what the yuffie becomes. Free-floating genius. But at the same time a grossly underpaid functionary or paper shuffler or peddler.

Luckily for the yuffie, while he may spend his days making someone else rich, at night he is home writing the great American novel or inventing the perpetual motion machine.

What the yuffie never learns—mercifully—is that *posthumous doesn't count.* (See Chapter Seventeen.)

ABD: "all but dissertation," as close as you can get to a Ph.D. without having to get out into the real world.

A comparison between yuppie jobs and yuffie jobs

yuppie	*yuffie*
brain surgeon	butcher in a natural foods store
corporate attorney	junior high civics teacher
architect	freelance house painter
civil engineer	bicycle repairman
interior designer	history museum curator
starlet	Summer Playhouse box office manager

PART TWO

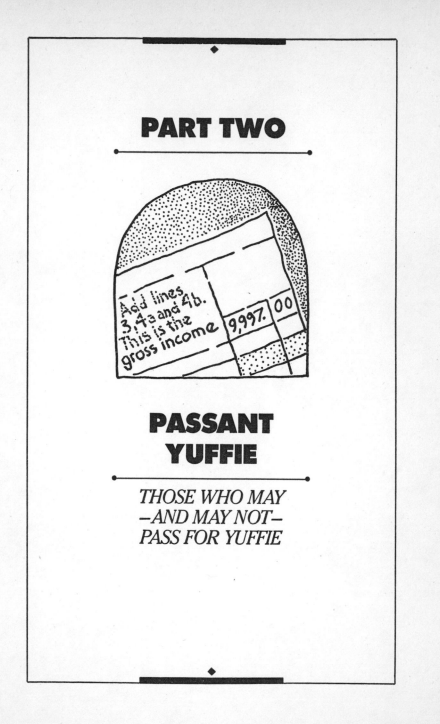

PASSANT
YUFFIE

*THOSE WHO MAY
–AND MAY NOT–
PASS FOR YUFFIE*

CHAPTER THREE

THE CLOSET YUFFIE

rony of ironies, yuffies as a group were born on Madison Avenue. It seems there was a whole slice of the American spending pie unaccounted for—the baby boomers who make less than $10,000 a year. Since everyone is a potential spender, it was inevitable that the marketing pundits would latch onto that poor, misbegotten segment of society. And a Mr. Lempert did. (He's one of those eternally successful types who probably woke up one morning, declared himself a marketing expert, and started a newsletter for which he charges more than a yuffie's weekly grocery bill.) Lempert slapped the label "yuffie" on the unlabeled piece of the pie graph, and the rest is history.

Ten thousand dollars! You have to be extremely adroit in ducking work to make less than ten thousand dollars. Especially when everyone you've ever known is a yuppie with business connections. The only zeal greater than that of a miserably married woman who likes to fix up friends on blind dates is the clock-puncher who wants to find the perfectly miserable job for his unemployed friends.

Ten thousand dollars! It's even harder to live on that than it is to avoid earning it.

So where are all these forty-year-old financial failures? Flipping burgers at McDonald's? Living out of shopping bags under the highway ramp? Well, maybe some are, but there are quite a few you'll find right there at the cocktail parties, the private

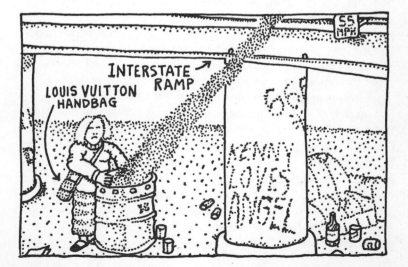

school parents' meetings, even looking as if they belong in the Volvo showroom.

These are the closet yuffies. They probably think they're yuppies. *Yuppies* probably think they're yuppies.

There obviously is only one way to survive as a closet yuffie, and that's to have an outside source of income. Closet yuffies are legion: how many wives of MDs have you ever met who earn over $10,000 a year?

Parents, husbands, wives, lovers, patronizing siblings: this is how the closet yuffie survives. Mummy and Daddy put him in trust until he's 30, and the day after his 30th birthday he starts clipping coupons. Of course, he tells anyone who asks—and if they don't ask, he volunteers it—that he's begun selling his photographs from his last trip to Nepal. That's where the sudden wealth comes from—the great success of his creative efforts. The closet yuffie, like anyone who lives in the closet, is an insufferable phony, at least to those of us who are right out there living with our label and proud of it.

That goes for the yuffie who passes for yuppie on spouse-wealth. Marrying an attorney or the terribly homely daughter of a real estate scion is not a world-class life achievement. The yuffie who is married to money and walks around in a t-shirt with Franz Kafka on the front and holds a Ph.D. in Comparative Literature and could hold a job but doesn't—now that's a bona fide yuffie, a fine member of the ranks. And also a rarity. The yuffie wears the emblem of failure with blazing arrogance—and the yuffie who's living at the mercy of spouse-wealth usually doesn't have permission for self-expression. How many Vice Presidents of Development and Administration have wives who show up at the office Christmas party in Birkenstock sandals?

Little is sadder than the closet yuffie who's living the good life on baby brother's investments. It goes something like this: the yuffie was probably the long-tortured middle child, the one caught in life's cruelest squeeze play. Failure is a way of life for middle children, or so psychologists say. (Though psychologists also say that third children are always the fanatically religious ones, and Lord knows there are not enough pulpits to go around if that's true.) So in their mutual growing up years, it was quite easy for little brother to be an easy school star: there was no precedent to beat. And little brother grew up to perfect the aperture flywheeled graumus, made a million bucks, and made big yuffie sister a do-nothing vice president of the corporation. Big sister goes to all the charity fashion shows and gives Sponsor-size sums to cure obscure diseases. Big sister is a closet yuffie. If she has a husband, he is probably Vice President in Charge of Graumus Marketing. And he is the most reprehensible closet yuffie of all.

With yuppie roots, the closet yuffie has unlimited opportunities to find quiet pools of money that he can pass off as the product of his own labors. Closet yuffies—gay or straight—are as drawn to the solvent lover as iron filings to an alnico magnet. Now if they were honest about their failure, proud of it, then they could leech to their hearts content. But they're not honest. That's why we say they're in the closet. Hey, look, go ask Mummy for $6.95, and get yourself a copy of this book. (A true yuffie would check it out of the library, but that's another story.)

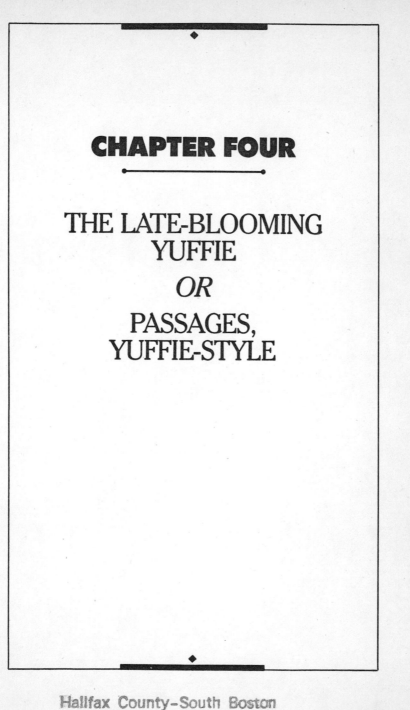

CHAPTER FOUR

THE LATE-BLOOMING YUFFIE

OR

PASSAGES, YUFFIE-STYLE

The 40th birthday—it's the biggest life trauma since your first zit. Pillars of the community have been known to do reprehensible things when they get to the peak, right before that fast slide down to you-know-what. Junior Leaguers get *jobs,* long-married men get fresh new nymphets.

And some, the wisest ones, choose to live out their declining years as yuffies. Run off to the Seychelles. Grow a beard and live on the beach and build 30-foot steel alloy sculptures. Open a bookstore specializing in opera libretti and books full of photographs of filling stations.

Neo-yuffies, late-blooming yuffies—they have the true trappings of failure. At least after their savings run out. And true yuffies, born to failure, are flattered by imitation and warmly welcome them to the ranks. *After* their savings run out.

The late-blooming yuffie has been on a rollercoaster ride to Ultimate Failure. He was a kid yuffie: but who knows you're a flub as a kid? (The flip side of that, of course, is what gives the born yuffie his humility: who knows you're a genius as a kid?) Ordinary, ordinary, ordinary—what could be worse?

Or better: with no neurotic mother crowing about his being the next Jack Kennedy, the late-blooming yuffie slid right into success in his teen years. He made good grades, he played varsity sports, he thought born yuffies were toads.

Ah, but the 20s. Those halcyon, democratic years. Except for the little snots who go to med school, law school, and business school, everyone flaps around aimlessly in his 20s, remember? Hard-core baby boomers probably put in their time on $244 a month helping their third-world brethren in the Peace Corps and VISTA—or struggling nobly through a Ph.D. in Sociology. All for the benefit of mankind. *And* for avoiding a one-way ticket to Vietnam. (Or, if they were female, trapping a do-gooder in a love liaison while he sweated out the war anywhere in the world except Southeast Asia.)

Thirty: time for success. Who can stand $244 a month forever? The soon-to-be late-blooming yuffie is back into his yuppie cycle. Account executive, market analyst, administrator of Granny's portfolio. The beautiful acquisitive years.

So what happens on the 40th birthday? Something trips the pleasure button. Probably all that outpouring of sympathy—those wine-sodden talks on the meaning of life. The late-blooming

NEO YUFFIE BEACH HOUSE: BEFORE & AFTER SAVINGS RUN OUT.

(BEFORE)

(AFTER)

TUNA

yuffie rediscovers the true pleasure passages of his earlier life in the throes of his mid-life crisis.

What could be more in tune with the aimless brilliance of the yuffie life than the polymorphous perversity of childhood? Ever watch a kid? Kids are little stoned people without the benefit of chemicals. They'll say anything that pops into their soft little skulls. They won't get out of bed in the morning unless something's in it for them. (Even if that something is only the thrill of bugging the bejeezus out of everyone else.) A natural yuffie life.

Same for the 20s—a time of *total* perversity. And feeling good. No wonder the late-blooming yuffie recaptures his youth. *His* youth doesn't seem so bad—when he's looked at the alternatives.

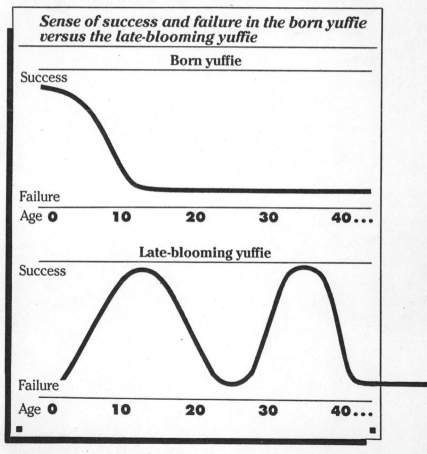

Sense of success and failure in the born yuffie versus the late-blooming yuffie

Born yuffie

Late-blooming yuffie

CHAPTER FIVE

SLUMMING—
THE WEEKEND
YUFFIE

Al Jolson in blackface was *not* cute. And anyone who mimics those he *thinks* are his social inferiors is equally uncute. So there's no flattery in the yuffie-imitation some yuppies do on weekends.

Such condescension! Such phonies! (The only phonies worse than weekend yuffies are closet yuffies.) They're just like the pinks-in-mink of the fifties, all those *grandes dames* who sent fat checks to the NAACP and hollered at their upstairs maids. In the eighties they get right out there and get grubby with the peons. The yuffies.

We're not even talking about that swell legion who write articles like "My Three Days as a Bag Lady" or "I Lived in a City Shelter for a Week." (They leave a cash-chocked wallet in a locker at the Port Authority and a car in a mid-town parking lot.)

No, we're talking about dabblers in squalor. The urologist who writes poems and recites them at the Maple Coffee House Sunday afternoons. (Drippy poems, of course.) He slurps on a pipe and wears ten-year-old docksiders and nurses an orange pekoe ice tea. And he looks very serious. Knows all the regulars on a first-name basis. Though if that ex-professor alcoholic who lives in the back room of the coffee house and oversees poetry readings ever gets a kidney stone, would the good doctor treat him? Not unless he had Medicaid.

Then there's the bank vice president who's been to enough gallery openings with his wife to get an urge to create. So he paints a 1962 Cadillac pink, buries the front end in his backyard (or the back end in his front yard, depending on how daring he is) and invites every starving artist in town over for canapes. But don't ask him who dug the hole.

Or the insurance broker who tells everyone who'll listen that he's written a novel. He actually has—600 pages (with half-inch margins) of a day in the life of an insurance broker. Leopold Bloom he's not. Lots of 38-D secretaries in high-rise elevators. Contemplations on the actuarial tables as they fit into the cosmos.

Weekend yuffies wear ragged clothes. But that sweater cost $85 at Harrod's five years ago. It'll go to the maid's husband when summer gets here.

Weekend yuffies always have a big stack of books lying around. Hardbacks with no dust jackets. They look terrific in piles like that—but they're actually by Sidney Sheldon.

Weekend yuffies love to run around taking photographs with a big fat 35-mm camera. But look closely: everything's automatic. Even the flow of cash to print 60 shots of a bridge taken from 500 yards without a telephoto lens. (Look carefully, it's that little gray spot up in the left-hand corner.)

Weekend yuffies love to say, "We've got tickets for tonight." Of course, they're either tickets to a basketball game or symphony tickets good for a three-hour nap in a tux. Weekend yuffies don't know Beethoven from Bartok, but they go to every annual Symphony Ball.

What's the fun of being a weekend yuffie? Ask one. But do it in private; it's only kind.

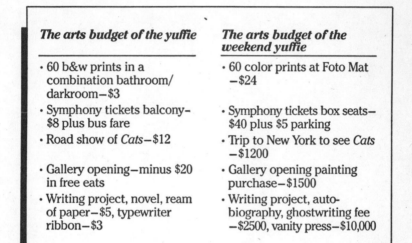

The arts budget of the yuffie	*The arts budget of the weekend yuffie*
• 60 b&w prints in a combination bathroom/darkroom—$3	• 60 color prints at Foto Mat —$24
• Symphony tickets balcony—$8 plus bus fare	• Symphony tickets box seats—$40 plus $5 parking
• Road show of *Cats*—$12	• Trip to New York to see *Cats* —$1200
• Gallery opening—minus $20 in free eats	• Gallery opening painting purchase—$1500
• Writing project, novel, ream of paper—$5, typewriter ribbon—$3	• Writing project, autobiography, ghostwriting fee —$2500, vanity press—$10,000

PART THREE

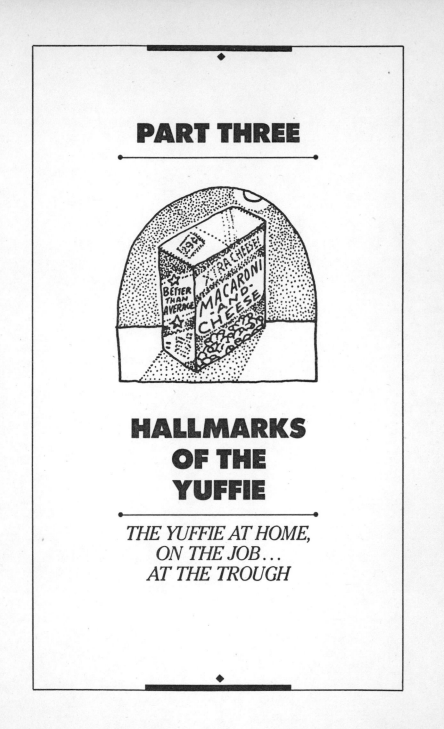

HALLMARKS
OF THE
YUFFIE

*THE YUFFIE AT HOME,
ON THE JOB...
AT THE TROUGH*

CHAPTER SIX

THE YUFFIE HABITAT

Yuffies are visionaries—even if their visions always work out for somebody else instead. All the most exquisite neighborhoods: yuffies discovered them first. Yuffies and gentrification don't go together: yuffies can't afford a whole lot of sheetrock and sandblasting. But yuffies *do* gravitate to the neighborhoods which are going to be yuppified five years down the road. They give the neighborhood cachet: knock down a few walls, hand-sand a few floors, hang a few 10 by 20 canvasses—then draw a coffeehouse, a natural foodstore, a bookshop. And before you know it, rents have tripled, and yuffies are loading 20 boxes of books into a U-Haul.

Look at SoHo. The Haight—well, hippies were nothing if not yuffies-in-training. (Don't mention Jerry Rubin and such.) Capitol Hill in half a dozen cities. Yuffies oozed all over Berkeley. And look at what's happened to the whole town of Santa Fe.

Yuffies always have terrific furniture. So what if your recliner is Uncle Harold's old dentist's chair? And your coffee table used to be the back door to your previous apartment building? Yuffies *never* buy furniture, unless it's mostly pillows and made in Japan.

Yuffie rules for home selection and decoration

1. Never live anywhere built after 1930.

2. Never live within five miles of a cul-de-sac.

3. Do not *buy* furniture, except at the futon store.

4. Never have two pieces of furniture which match.

5. Always get triple the square footage you'd get for your rent in a yuppie neighborhood.

6. Never frame anything. Thumbtacks and scotch tape are fine. (You may hang framed works if they are gifts.)

7. You can upholster anything—including walls—with a staple gun and an old sheet.

8. Dust semi-annually. The stuff's going to come back anyway.

9. You may not own a dishwasher or microwave oven. It's unprincipled.

THE YUFFIE LIVING ROOM.

MAP OF TOGO.

PITHY QUOTE FROM GOGOL.

BIRDCAGE, RESURRECTED FROM GRANNY'S ATTIC IN IOWA.

PLASTER COPY OF GREEK BRONZE, INHERITED FROM DECEASED AND MISERLY UNCLE.

SMALL PART OF 1,000-WATT STEREO SYSTEM.

"FAKE FUR" ZEBRASKIN PILLOW.

CHAIR, BOUGHT AT MOTEL BANKRUPTCY AUCTION: $4.50

"SWANN'S WAY," MODERN LIBRARY EDITION.

YEARBOOK DEPRESSION ERA, FROM RURAL DUST BOWL HIGH SCHOOL.

GLASS AND CHROME COFFEE TABLE, DISCO ERA, SALVAGED FROM NIGHTCLUB DYNAMITED BY MAFIA.

SOFA, ON LOAN FROM YUPPIE SIBLING WHO'S JOB-HUNTING IN CALIFORNIA.

Yuffies know Parkinson's Law of Furniture: *the volume of furniture expands to fill the space allotted to it.* There's always more furniture floating around the world in moving vans than there are houses to take it all in. Yuffies always have relatives who die at convenient times. And with classy roots, yuffies inherit classy furniture. (Even if it is the leavings after aggressive cousins have walked off with the Rouaults and the genuine Breuers.) Friends who fall off the material end of the earth and move into ashrams and communes often bequeath fine stuff to yuffie friends—unless they liquidate to help pay off their guru's Rolls. And there's always an occasional yuffie to get a grandfather clock on *Wheel of Fortune.*

One thing yuffies never stint: their stereos. A yuffie may have a black and white portable TV with aluminum foil on the antenna. (Cable? Horrors, no.) A yuffie may have to flip the ball every time he flushes the toilet. The yuffie may have a crack in his bedroom ceiling to rival the San Andreas Fault. But the yuffie has a Bang & Olufsson stereo. Or is working up to one.

Not all yuffies are renters. Yuffies who were resigned to their fates may have bought houses back in 1975 when all it took was a down payment of $4000 and $150 a month. House upkeep is a special challenge to the yuffie. The yuffie waits until the rotting roof overhang falls off to save on the labor of having it pulled down. The yuffie refuses to believe electrical wiring and plumbing have anything to do with him personally. His landscape architectural concept is straight out of *Suddenly Last Summer.* And the yuffie does not cut his grass until he's stepped in something three times.

Acceptable items for a yuffie bathroom or kitchen

- pithy quotes typed on yellowing paper, taped to the wall
- photos of Andy Kaufman torn from magazines, taped to the wall
- postcards bought in museum shops, taped to the wall
- topographical maps of obscure parts of the world, taped to the wall
- bare light bulb
- ScotTissue 1000-sheet roll

Unacceptable items for a yuffie bathroom or kitchen

- framed pressed flowers
- kitchen witch
- anything Early American
- liquid soap
- dimmer switch
- colored toilet paper
- colored paper towels
- refrigerator magnets

CHAPTER SEVEN

THE YUFFIE
FEEDING HABITS
OR
CAN VERSUS BRAN

The yuffie personality—Type Y—has that one important characteristic which guarantees long life. A phlegmatic attitude. Yuffies figure, Why bother with health when you've already got it? Yuffies usually have a cholesterol count of 150, without trying. That's why yuffies never exercise—and that's why yuffies don't care what they eat. As long as it's easy. The feeding rule for yuffies is simple: *never prepare anything which takes longer to cook than to eat.*

And shopping for food is the first part of cooking. The yuffie has one supermarket for all his needs. (Though he has no aversion to buying groceries in a drugstore or convenience store. In fact, yuffies who live within a block of a convenience store have been known to live an entire week on frosted flakes, canned beef stew, and icees.)

Yuffies never comparison shop. Grocery ads are for stuffing cracks under the door in winter. And this business of hopping from vegetable stand to bakery to butcher—very continental, but *very* boring. If it hasn't got a UPC, it isn't worth having.

Price doesn't matter. The yuffie never looks at the prices on a shelf—he buys the brand name with the highest logo recognition. He just spends until the money runs out. And the yuffie doesn't use coupons: a few dimes are not worth the output of mental energy.

Grocery lists are for philistines. Yuffies prefer spontaneity: if it doesn't sing out from the shelf, it's not on the menu for the week. Yuffies may be cash poor, but they're the stuff of which market research dreams are made. Yuffies prefer labels with red and yellow on them: they brighten up a kitchen.

The yuffie never cooks from scratch. To the yuffie, adding the milk and butter to the macaroni and cheese is a *cordon bleu* achievement.

This is not to say that fresh foods never cross a yuffie's lips. A yuffie will eat an entire green pepper, but he'd never chop it up and drop it in a roux.

The expenditure of brain power on the feeding process is to be avoided by the yuffie. That's why the yuffie serves only the wine someone gave him last Christmas. It's why he can spell radicchio and arugula, but can't be bothered with figuring out what they are. And it's why *most* yuffies can go no further in the pursuit of vegetarianism than to down a box of Cracker Jacks for

lunch. Being the contemplative sort, the yuffie usually abhors the slaughter of animals for food. Being the phlegmatic sort, the yuffie is usually too distracted to try to figure out seven different ways to cook tofu. Tofu doesn't come in cans, and eating raw, unvarnished tofu is a sure route to tossing one's blackstrap molasses cookies.

There are exceptions to the rule. It's a carryover from the high school years, when every yuffie was entitled to a single, overriding passion. (Remember: an A-plus in Conversational Sanskrit was okay as long as all your other grades were Ds.) And *some* grown yuffies are vegetarians, because all true vegetarians are yuffies. They're in it for the animals. An excellent passion.

Why are all true vegetarians yuffies? Quite simple: they *look* like yuffies. And can you picture a yuppie passing up sushi?

CHAPTER EIGHT

YUFFIE PARENTHOOD: THE QUICK ROAD TO ABJECT POVERTY

Yuffies know that having children is the fastest route to financial ruin. And since financial ruin is the hallmark of being a yuffie, yuffies who have kids always have at least one too many.

(Of course, a great number of yuffies do not have children; it does require an expenditure of energy. But those yuffies know that they are truly working toward ultimate poverty, ensured for a lifetime. Who's going to bring them chicken soup and place them in a home when they're sixty-four? Not having children gives the yuffie every promise of becoming a bag lady.)

Embarking on parenthood is deceptively cheap for the yuffie. The first years cost the yuffie almost nothing. As the old saying goes, God looks after children and damn fools. Since there are several of each in a yuffie household, childbirth always goes smoothly for the yuffie couple—no complications. So they get bargain basement rates at the hospital. Yuffie offspring are always breastfed: remember, a yuffie will never cook anything which takes longer to prepare than to eat. A yuffie mother simply snarfs down a box of Cracker Jacks, and she's ready to feed the kid.

And most of all, yuffies' babies are cheap to keep because of…GRANDPARENTS! Mummy and Daddy right away spot a new generation ripe for redeeming the family name. So the yuffie offspring gets a practical nurse for two weeks (Mummy is *not* one for changing diapers and sleeping on a cot waiting for the 3 a.m. feeding). Baby gets a complete set of size 0 hand-knit sweaters, even if it's born in July. Feltman suits are *de rigueur,* even when Baby starts dragging those crisp whites across a dusty floor. Florence Eiseman dresses hang on the rack three years early. Mummy gets everything monogrammed—or has the poor kid's name appliqueed down his front in five colors of calico. (Thank goodness yuffies give their kids unpronounceable names, or they'd be sure to be kidnapped.)

And Mummy springs for every ridiculous geegaw on the market. Johnny Jump-Up and Swyngomatic and Crib Cuddle—all those contraptions to keep you from holding the kid, things she wishes had been invented in 1946.

Mummy keeps it up: anything which flies in the face of the yuffie lifestyle pours forth from Mummy's coffers. Mummy promises to pay for Baby's education through medical school. So

Baby goes to the most exclusive nursery school—the one on the Harvard track. And Baby makes it into the most exclusive private kindergarten, one more step along the Harvard track. Then Mummy gets bored shelling out $5000 a year, says she's having cash flow problems, and Baby goes on scholarship. Luckily for Baby, the IQ's in the genes. Baby'll go to Harvard and medical school on his own hook: he's already earning his way, and he's only six.

The result: yuppiehood is going to skip a generation. The pendulum swings: Granny was a flapper who got thrown out of college for smoking cigarettes. Mummy is a society matron who married at 21 and gets her hair done once a week. Yuffie is yuffie. And Yuffie's kid is going to rebel in the one way he knows

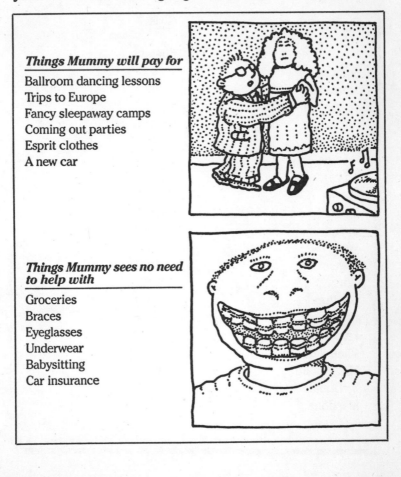

Things Mummy will pay for

Ballroom dancing lessons
Trips to Europe
Fancy sleepaway camps
Coming out parties
Esprit clothes
A new car

Things Mummy sees no need to help with

Groceries
Braces
Eyeglasses
Underwear
Babysitting
Car insurance

will kill his parents. Not drugs. Not bad grades. Not low-life friends. His parents already tried all that. But *success*. His parents won't be able to face their friends.

They've given him a literary name. They've played Peter, Paul, and Mary albums next to his crib. They've taken him to Animal Peace vigils. And the kid's going to drop his name for an initial, get rich—and raise his own yuffie.

Acceptable names for yuffie children

Boys	Girls
Dashiell	Eustacia
Somerset	Tess
Sinclair	Esme
Sherwood	Maisie
Rudyard	Ursula
Ogden	Gudrun
Erskine	Odette
Tristan	Ada
Travis	Rowena
Dylan	Clea
Evelyn	Cordelia
Walker	Ophelia
Fraser	Desdemona
Gore	Anais
Geoffrey	Carson
Graham	Eudora
Langston	Simone
Chandler	Germaine
MacDonald	Flannery
McDonald	
Macdonald	

CHAPTER NINE

THE WELL-DRESSED YUFFIE

he yuffie dresses one of two ways: underdress or under duress. So he has two wardrobes. One he wears daily, and one he wears on oppressive occasions. Of course, oppressive occasions can last for months—in those cases the yuffie generally goes nuts from being a phony for hours on end.

The yuffie does not believe in clothes making a statement—even if it's one of contempt.

The yuffie just wears clothes because they're there. As a result, he's always one step out of sync with fashion cycles. Yuffies were wearing luau shirts from the Goodwill—until Jams came in. Now yuffies are wearing shirts with little alligators on them—just like everyone else living below the poverty line.

Left to his own devices, the yuffie would simply cover the necessary parts of his body, depending on season. (Extra flab or skinny limbs make no difference to a yuffie: fat only counts if it's between your ears.) Season is a personal thing: a yuffie might very well wear sandals in Chicago in March.

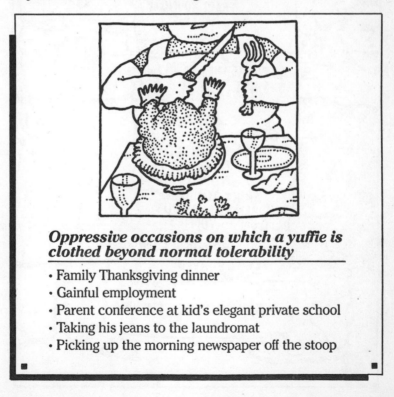

Oppressive occasions on which a yuffie is clothed beyond normal tolerability

- Family Thanksgiving dinner
- Gainful employment
- Parent conference at kid's elegant private school
- Taking his jeans to the laundromat
- Picking up the morning newspaper off the stoop

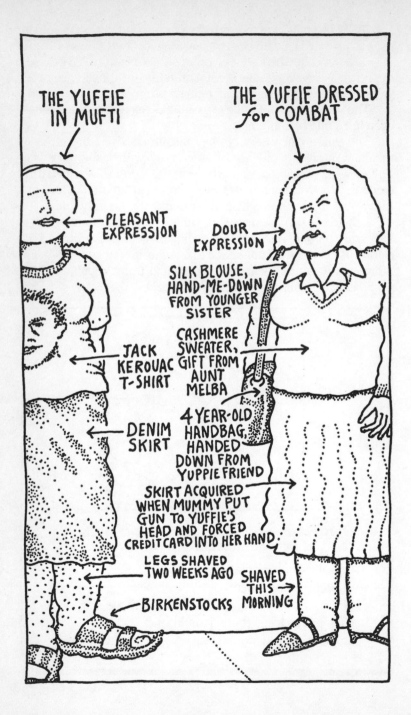

And speaking of season, color selection by complexion is one of life's finest absurdities to the yuffie. The yuffie color choice is like the Luscher color test. By mood. Though yuffie moods are usually winter colors. Black or white, depending on how he is faring existentially. That's why the yuffie's favorite color often appears to be gray: the yuffie believes in only doing one load of laundry at a time. Mercifully, he also does not believe in Clorox.

The mainstay of the yuffie wardrobe is one pair of pants. Usually designer denim, compliments of Mummy's largesse. After several weekly washings, these go well with all his t-shirts. The yuffie buys his t-shirts from Historical Products: he prefers pictures of Albert Camus, T.S. Eliot, William Faulkner, F. Scott Fitzgerald, Ernest Hemingway, James Joyce, Vladimir Nabokov, Marcel Proust, and Jean-Paul Sartre. All the guys who, if alive today, would be doing American Express commercials.

Some shirts the yuffie gets from his urbane, well-traveled yuppie friends. A yuffie will wear a t-shirt from the Hard Rock Cafe in London, just to confuse everybody.

The yuffie is too phlegmatic to Dress for Failure. (The yuffie has other, more noble ways to express his attitude toward the world of work and upward mobility.) When faced with self-righteous, authoritarian, oppressive, power-wielding, cloying sorts like mothers, bosses, and yuppie friends who offer to treat to lunch—the yuffie gives in easily. No problem. For the yuffie has another wardrobe.

In the creation of the Dress for Oppression wardrobe, the yuffie lives by one rule: *wear only gifts and hand-me-downs*. Here's what the yuffie usually hears right before he has to go scrounging for an extra hanger:

- "I'll treat you to an Easter suit."
- "I've got a pile of stuff for the Goodwill if you want to take a look first."
- "I found you the cutest little dress at Marshall's, and it was only $39."
- "I won't be needing this sweater this year in the Bahamas."

So the yuffie's state occasion wardrobe is quite a stylish collection—two years out of date.

Here's what yuffies have always done: wear only cotton. Here's what yuffies have never done: iron.

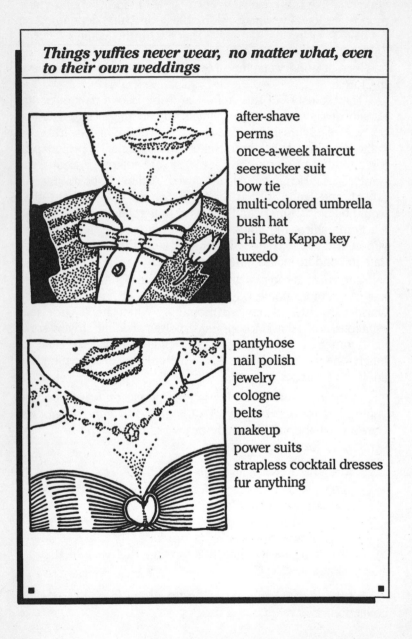

Things yuffies never wear, no matter what, even to their own weddings

after-shave
perms
once-a-week haircut
seersucker suit
bow tie
multi-colored umbrella
bush hat
Phi Beta Kappa key
tuxedo

pantyhose
nail polish
jewelry
cologne
belts
makeup
power suits
strapless cocktail dresses
fur anything

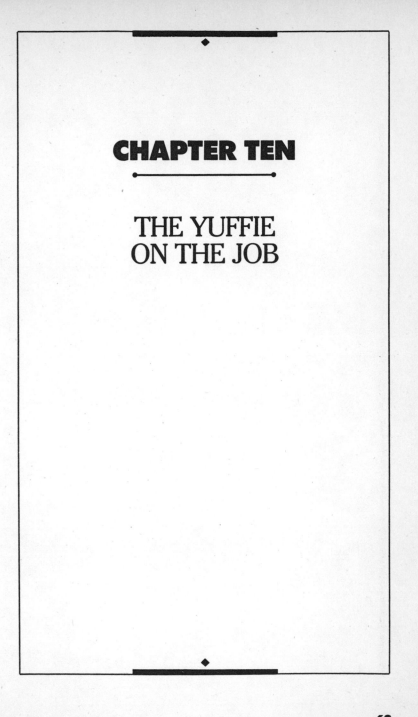

CHAPTER TEN

THE YUFFIE
ON THE JOB

n the workplace, the yuffie defies the Peter Principle: he hangs in just below his level of competence. That means he's probably the smartest person doing his job in the whole organization. And either too smart to be loosed from under the oppressor's thumb—or too smart to seek more responsibility.

What do all yuffie vocations have in common? They involve beating one's head up against a wall all day. Sisyphus is the patron saint of yuffies on the job: rolling that rock up the hill until 4:59, then watching it roll back down again at 5:00, so you have to start over tomorrow. With the guarantee of never amounting to anything. Never having an impact. Failure.

Salary is a particularly sensitive issue with the yuffie. Money is, in the general scheme in which yuffies are forced to live, the grand measure of one's worth. Having been told he was worthless (if brilliant) since junior high, the yuffie needs a salary which reflects his merit. Which is zilch. And so the yuffie negotiates:

"I'd consider the job for $6 an hour."
"How about $5.50?"
"Would you settle for $5?"

A potential employer who sees through this clever ruse and goes back up to $5.50 will be put off politely with a "can I let you know tomorrow?"

For the ideal boss for the yuffie is a mixture of Simon Legree and his own mother. The yuffie must remain shackled to his desk. Beaten down by the bureaucracy. With just enough elasticity in the authority structure for the yuffie occasionally to slip and try his brains out. He may develop an extra cog for the aperture flywheeled graumus which will increase profits 300 percent. What's he get? A memo reminding him that he's three months behind on his filing.

Labor as he may, or may not, the yuffie gets few fringe benefits on the job: one week's vacation after a year; Labor Day, Thanksgiving, and Christmas off; and a six-pound chicken for Christmas. Yuffies do not get life insurance, dental insurance, major medical insurance, sick leave, pension plans, or corporate cars. Yuffies are never unionized. That's partly because yuffies think unions are for greedy dummies, and partly because yuffies are too ill-defined job-wise to know which union to join.

Yuffies hate their jobs, but they don't take them personally.

They're a way to log eight hours on a payroll—so the yuffie can come home at night and turn to his *art*. The yuffie will never achieve fame and fortune at the Wheelwright Aperture Flywheeled Graumus Corporation. But that 1000-page tome in his desk drawer at home: there's his immortality. Even if it never sees print until he's been dead a hundred years. A quaint period piece, that's how they'll see it. But who cares?

PART FOUR

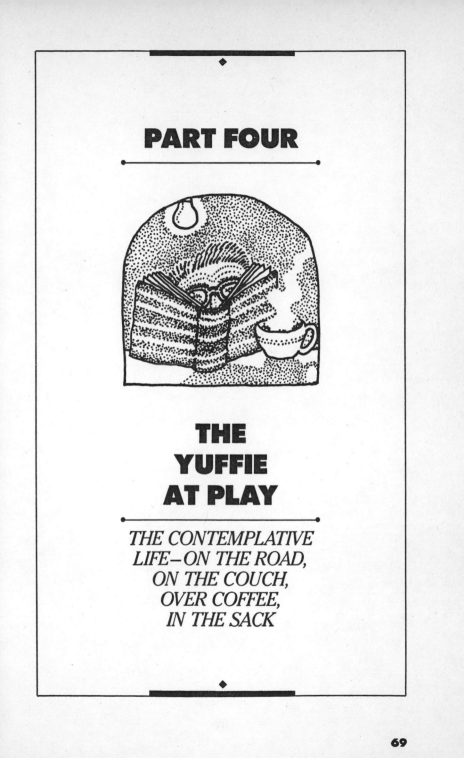

THE
YUFFIE
AT PLAY

*THE CONTEMPLATIVE
LIFE–ON THE ROAD,
ON THE COUCH,
OVER COFFEE,
IN THE SACK*

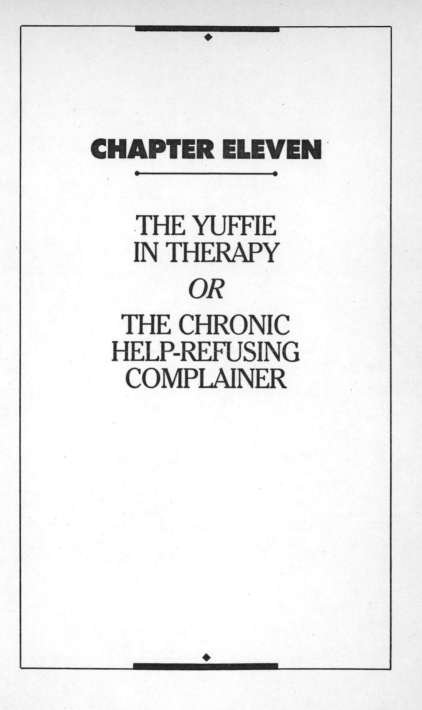

CHAPTER ELEVEN

THE YUFFIE IN THERAPY

OR

THE CHRONIC HELP-REFUSING COMPLAINER

Until this book came out, yuffiehood was always a source of shame. Failure: it *sounds* pejorative. Like a brand on you for your sins, or a social deviation. It's taken until now, with the rise of yuffie pride, for the failure option to be one of the saner ways to go through life.

So the yuffie probably has an early history of sitting in fake Queen Anne chairs under monochromatic paintings of seascapes, right next to fake Louis XIV coffeetables with fancy boxes of blue kleenex in the middle. And the requisite portraits of a lovely wife and 2.4 children on an otherwise bare mahogany desk.

With zany, freethinking parents, the yuffie probably saw his first psychiatrist at age 12. Sessions began shortly after an IQ test and a few psychological exams. The young yuffie strove for creativity in these tests, giving the noble examiner some entertainment variety on such matters as number recall. Despite his efforts to skew his scores into meaninglessness, he came out with a damning IQ of 158 and was promptly packed off to Dr. Cohen. (Half of all psychiatrists and gynecologists are named Dr. Cohen.)

For fifty minutes every Wednesday afternoon, when everyone else had piano lessons or football practice, the young yuffie entertained Dr. Cohen. It was easy to do—it was Daddy's money.

Finally, when graduation approached, college plans were finalized, and Dr. Cohen's Cadillac was paid off, Dr. Cohen proferred his diagnosis. "This kid is a chronic, help-refusing complainer," he announced solemnly to your mother, while you listened in on the kitchen extension.

Conversational gambits guaranteed to keep Dr. Cohen in stony silence

- "Isn't free association fun?"
- "Last night I dreamed I was drowning in a box of corn flakes."
- "Read anything by Sophocles lately?"
- "I've decided that my ego ideal is Dorothy Parker."
- "I burned a cross on Henry Horowitz's lawn Saturday night."

The cynicism evaporated in your early 20s. That's when everyone made The Great Discovery (during the era when everyone belonged to The Panacea of the Month Club): you could go into five-day-a-week analysis for $2 a pop—as a guinea pig for residents in analysis at the med school. Hey, you reasoned, this is more fun than amyl nitrate! And longer lasting, too!

And so began the long, serious career of the Chronic Help-Refusing Complainer. Your analysis at the med school didn't last until you were stripped bare of your defenses and healthily built up to new ways of coping. No, your analysis lasted until:

1. Your doctor got his certification and went on to charge $50 an hour, dropping you like a hot potato,
2. Your doctor discovered in his own analysis that he was gay and went off to Colorado, or
3. You got so nutsy in his OJT (on-the-job-training) that *you* went off to Colorado.

So what's the yuffie to do when, faced with an ache for formal self-probing (and self-pity), he can't afford $75 an hour? He's got this urge to be locked in a room with someone who has to listen to thoughts on failure for 50 minutes.

Most yuffies go for cheap. The yuffie learned about sliding scale back when he was a laboratory animal at the med school. And sliding scale means about $5 a session for the average yuffie.

Usually the yuffie's perfectly happy to babble away at a social worker. Social workers have just as much training as psychiatrists. Who counts those four years studying human plumbing? All it's worth is The Right to Write Prescriptions— and if the yuffie wants to pop fun drugs he can find them on the street, or suck them up his nose in yuppie-friends' bathrooms.

Social work is one of the great yuffie occupations. And yuffies love to patronize their peers. So what if half your sessions are filled with your therapist's hints about her happy childhood? Her romantic wedding? Her excellent academic career? Social workers know they're supposed to be totally neutral, faded into the woodwork. And social workers remind you every few sentences.

"You're curious about my family, aren't you?"

"I guess you noticed this ring I'm wearing. Why are you resisting talking about it?"

"I understand how you might be angry that I'm going on vacation and abandoning you."

Two exceptions to the choice of the social worker as therapist: one, the unbroken chain of psychiatrists. Some yuffies got so accustomed to seeing a psychiatrist in their youths that they have stayed in treatment all their adult lives. The yuffie may be earning $30,000 a year, but he's paying enough to Dr. Cohen's successor to be sure he stays below poverty level. Two, group therapy. Group therapy is full of yuffies. It's often their main form of social contact.

The day you can give your therapist the raspberry, you're cured. But therapy is something else yuffies fail at. Yuffies always give credence to their therapists. It's another great lapse of intelligence for the sake of failure.

The fundamental axiom of seeing a therapist

If your therapist weren't such a dismal failure himself, he'd be out on the street doing normal things.

CHAPTER TWELVE

THE YUFFIE AT LEISURE

OR

THE FINE ART OF COFFEE-DRINKING AND KILLING TIME

Here's what the yuffie hates: *kaffeeklatsches*. Here's. what the yuffie loves: getting together over coffee—especially when he's alone.

The yuffie takes his coffee-making seriously: coffee is the one consumable substance which takes longer to finish off than to fix (see Chapter Seven on the feeding habits of yuffies). The yuffie has a squeeze pot, a drip pot, and an espresso machine. He's found a coffeehouse undiscovered by yuppies. And he's got a fine collection of fellow yuffies who can do coffee on a moment's notice. The yuffie does coffee with *somebody* at least three times a week. And every other day he goes and sits in the coffeehouse with a copy of *Godel Escher Bach* in front of him and stares into space until his coffee gets cold.

But coffee-drinking can't fill a whole day—every nervous system has its limits. Yet not earning money buys the yuffie much leisure time. Which he spends in the splendid pastime called "Collecting for Fun and No Profit."

Here's how to play "Collecting for Fun and No Profit."

Step 1—Buy a book or classical record (depending on which is your pleasure intake sense). Go to a reputable second-hand bookshop or classical record store. You want to buy from experts who know how to price merchandise. A flea market or junk shop might produce bargains. *Bargains run counter to the yuffie lifestyle.*

Step 2—Love it half to death. Wear those grooves down, drop peanut butter and jelly on those pages.

Step 3—Don't keep it long. Everything appreciates with age—except an American-made car.

Step 4—Put it in a pile with all the others you've been accumulating in the corner of the bathroom.

Step 5—Place a "25 cents" sticker on it, cart if over to your sister-in-law's garage sale, and unload it.

Congratulations: you've shot about 20 hours and tallied a neat $9.75 loss—and you're no more materially encumbered than you were when you started.

Taking in culture: it's the mainstay of the free-floating genius.

Yuffies hang out in second-hand bookshops and cruise classical record stores—and yuffies go to the movies. But only if they're

—in black and white, or
—subtitled, or both.

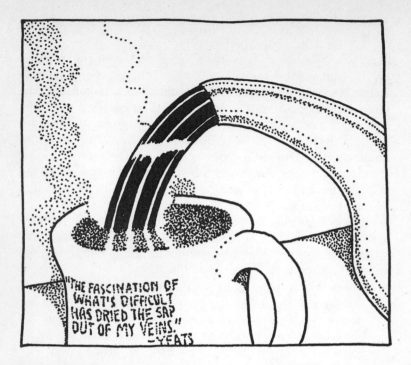

"THE FASCINATION OF WHAT'S DIFFICULT HAS DRIED THE SAP OUT OF MY VEINS."
—YEATS

What's okay with coffee

- beans of polysyllabic origin
- renaissance music
- a good argument over some arcane literature to spur the peristaltic process
- caffeine

What's not okay with coffee

- gossip
- talking about child-rearing
- talking about clothes
- talking about supermarket sales
- playing cards
- mah jongg
- talking about sports
- artificial sweetener

The Oscars are as full of familiar faces to a yuffie as the crowd scene in *Godzilla.* Yuffies have never heard of Meryl Streep. The rallying film of yuffies is *A Thousand Clowns,* even if Jason Robards (Murray Burns) does get a job at the end. Every yuffie has one dark summer in his past when he saw every film playing in town twice, even the Disney productions. (It was the summer he had an apartment with no air conditioning—and nowhere else to go during the day.)

As leisure-killing goes, yuffies have to be more creative than yuppies. Why? Well, haven't you ever noticed how much time yuppies spend on their bodies? *Yuffies never exercise on purpose.* They may bicycle, they may walk—but it's only because those are ways to get places without looking for a place to park.

Yuffies' favorite lines from movies

"Nick, in a moment you're going to see a horrible thing. People going to work."—Murray Burns, *A Thousand Clowns*

"I never answer letters from large organizations." —Murray Burns, *A Thousand Clowns*

"All the really important jobs stay forever."—Murray Burns, *A Thousand Clowns*

"With all these successful people around, where are all of our new young failures going to come from?" —Murray Burns, *A Thousand Clowns*

CHAPTER THIRTEEN

THE YUFFIE VACATION, NOT STARRING CHEVY CHASE

Everyone loves a yuffie. Yuffies always are thinking about things no one else is thinking of: they're terrific company. So certainly no one minds feeding and housing a yuffie for a week or two.

That's why the yuffie goes college-mate hopping whenever he leaves town. His roommate's probably laboring as a law firm partner in a downtown office of some visitable city. His senior tutor's probably off farming in rural Vermont. His sophomore girl friend is probably married to an absurdly secure six-figures-maker ten miles from a scenic desert.

The yuffie is a splendid house guest. He arrives with a ten-pound box of chocolates for his hostess, who's 20 pounds up since college. A Robbe-Grillet novel for her husband, the mono-syllabic ophthalmologist. And a Play Doh Fuzzy Pumper Pet Shop for the two-year-old. He makes his bed every day, including the day he leaves. And he never fools around with the hostess's nineteen-year-old sister.

Except for Humbert Humbert, no one's ever found the American scape fascinating for terribly long. So the ever-questing yuffie occasionally gets an urge to explore exotic lands. It's hard

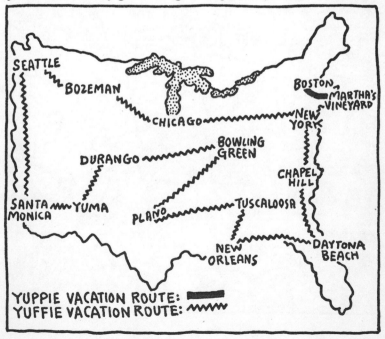

YUFFIE'S EXOTIC VACATION.

MANAGUA

to do a sponge vacation across international borders—unless you went to college with a bumper crop of CIA-aspirants.

So the yuffie usually immerses himself in the richness of foreign cultures by heading out on the Pan American Highway. Surely he'll find some yuppie who's happy to take him deep-sea fishing off Acapulco.

The yuffie is mildly air phobic. In part that's because he was so precious as a child that his raving neurotic mother never let him travel without advance prayers and rituals. (His mother would cancel a reservation if she dropped a knife at dinner. His mother invented the first seat belt in 1953 using 30 feet of clothesline.) Now, of course, his mother couldn't care less. As long as she's not the one flying.

And in part it's because the yuffie never can afford to travel by air often enough to get inured to airplane noises. Every groan means an imminent dive into a tract of ranch houses. Every crackle of the microphone means Prepare to Ditch in the Bay. And every small air pocket means sure death.

So the yuffie sticks to the interstates. Unless he gets an irresistible invitation across the Atlantic. Then he'll fly Icelandic. Icelandic is the official yuffie airline.

Packing for emergencies

Match what remedies yuffies pack (column A) for what emergencies (column B)

A	B
1. dental floss	a. the distributor cap gets wet
2. plastic garbage bag	b. your swimsuit rips
3. case of Cracker Jacks	c. you pick up a traveling companion
4. Motel 6 travel guide	d. all else fails
5. package of Gainesburgers	e. you run out of food
6. stapler	f. the tent collapses

1.f 2.a 3.e 4.d 5.c 6.b.

Things yuffies will do on vacation

- Get jellyfish stings
- Visit homes of obscure literary figures
- Eat three days straight at Burger King
- Sleep on the beach

- Camp in the Rockies
- Run out of cash
- Think
- Find sand dollars on the beach
- Send letters full of revelations which came during a walk at sunrise

Things yuffies never do on vacation

- Get tan
- Go places with several flags over them
- Eat in a restaurant with lots of ferns
- Stay in hotels more than two stories high
- Ski
- Use travelers checks
- Get bored
- Buy shells at souvenir stands

- Send scenic postcards

CHAPTER FOURTEEN

THE YUFFIE LIBRARY

When the yuffie moves—and some yuffies move semi-annually— he has one box of clothes, one box of kitchen paraphernalia, and 20 boxes of books.

Books have been at the center of the yuffie's life since infancy. Other babies played in the kitchen banging pots around; the yuffie-to-be was gumming pages out of Daddy's *Harvard Classics.* When other little kids were flexing their gonads on romance comic book angst, the yuffie-to-be was reading J.D. Salinger. In high school, while everyone else was whining and cursing over *David Copperfield,* the yuffie was negotiating alternate credit for having plowed through *Finnegan's Wake.*

Books stick to yuffies. The yuffie probably owns every book he's had since he was 12—except those he's tried to sell off in his annual purge (see Chapter Twelve re how to play "Collecting for Fun and No Profit"). The yuffie's still got his *Swann's Way* with embarrassing yellow highlighting from when he took Idea and Form in 1966. Somehow the yuffie has managed to collect about 80 percent of the Modern Library collection—though no two are shelved together.

> ### The yuffie alternatives to the Dewey Decimal and Library of Congress cataloging systems
>
> - by color
> - by size
> - by donor
> - by alphabetical order of titles
> - by chronological order of acquisition
> - by where they fell when last read

Since every book ever written has been read by some yuffie (even if it's only the author's spouse), yuffie literary preferences are hard to pinpoint. One fact seems clear, though: always one to foster posthumous glory, the yuffie prefers his writers dead. Especially dead in a hotel room with a gin bottle. Ernest Hemingway, F. Scott Fitzgerald, D. H. Lawrence, almost anyone who ever ate lunch at the Algonquin: these are the writers yuffies feel a funny kinship with.

YUFFIE LIBRARY

YUPPIE LIBRARY

Any book which has come out since 1970 is not in the yuffie's collection.* The yuffie is always one to yearn for another era: most yuffies wonder why they were not alive in the 1920s. So the yuffie sees anything written since *Trout Fishing in America* as vapid and derivative.

There is a major exception to this rule: a yuffie will happily add an autographed first edition of a new book to his collection. And this happens more often than one might suppose. Remember, yuffies waft in and out of yuppiedom just because yuffies are such delightful relics of the yuppie's youth. And even though yuppies can read about as well as yuffies can balance their checkbooks, yuppies love to look literate. Knowing new writers is a must for your average yuppie: look in any line at an autographing party, and you'll see more Laura Ashleys and Ralph Laurens than you see at your average Easter service at the High Episcopal Church. The yuffie usually gets his copy from a yuppie friend, reads it in secret, then sells it off to a dealer five years later. By then either the writer has faded into obscurity and his book isn't worth the space it occupies, or the writer has skyrocketed to fame and his book is a collector's item, good for 20 bucks toward a Faulkner first edition.

When book ownership gets tiresome, yuffies head for the library. Any library. The yuffie will sit on the floor of the stacks of the university library for a whole day—even if he's not enrolled there and never graduated. In the middle of the day, the yuffie clamors for space with bored housewives at the public library. When the yuffie moves to a new town, he gets a library card before he gets a driver's license or check-cashing card for the supermarket. The yuffie uses his library card until the card disintegrates—usually in the pocket of his jeans when they go through the wash. That's just about when the yuffie is changing addresses again, so it all works out just fine.

---

* There are only two books written after 1970 which are permissible. *Godel Escher Bach* came out in 1979, but it's okay— two out of three are now dead. *The Tao of Physics,* well, what can we say? It's not vapid or derivative.

CHAPTER FIFTEEN

SEX
AND THE
YUFFIE

The yuffie is looking for mental gymnastics in bed. Forget the *Jataveshtitaka* and *Kshiraniraka* and everything in between: the yuffie's *Kama Sutra* is more likely to come out of a book by Eric Berne. SWYMD, NIGYSOB* —they're just as unpronounceable— and a lot more fun.

Accustomed to failure, the yuffie can never quite adjust to what always amounts to overwhelming success in the sack. So he plays mind games just to keep up the expectation of failure.

The yuffie is perfectly satisfied with missionary-style bouncing around. No frills and contortions—things yuppies probably would do to make themselves worthy of comment, if they weren't so tired after working twelve-hour days. Yuffies like to believe their scripts are written by Woody Allen: all the yuffie wants is memorable dialogue.

Or an interruption which is equally unforgettable. A lovemaking session is quite complete for the yuffie if:
- the smoke detector goes off
- the boss phones
- the Jehovah's Witnesses ring the bell
- the kid walks in

Tension, tension, tension. Yuffies just love sexual tension. No one has dripped with as much sexual tension as the yuffie since Tristan and Iseult.

Jean-Paul Belmondo always smoked a cigarette after a good romp in bed. Yuffies crave something more cranial—and cheaper.

In coupling patterns, yuffies have it all over everybody else: yuffies have the leisure time to be monomaniacal about the quest. Yuffies never go to bistros for pickups. Too pedestrian, and too expensive. Yuffies never get fixed up on blind dates by well-meaning aunts: no one can tout a yuffie as a good prospect. Yuffies rarely meet lovers on the job—yuffies try not to stay long enough to catch last names, much less social diseases.

So yuffies go for love in all the romantic ways. Backing into him at the bargain book table. Dropping a cup of hot Colombian Supremo one foot from her chair at the coffeehouse. Rear-ending his VW at the light.

Unfortunately, most yuffies can't tell the difference between

---

*"See What You Made Me Do" and "Now I Got You You Son of a Bitch," from *Games People Play,* copyright 1964, Ballantine Books, one of the last great pre-1970 books.

the serious and the sublime. Failure can be assured by giving a gift on the wrong occasion—or to the very person who's allergic to it, horrified by it, or, worst, humiliated to death by it.

Ultimately, yuffies fall into four sexual categories:
- —straight
- —gay
- —married
- —all of the above.

Failure is an equal opportunity syndrome, which does not discriminate on the basis of the degree to which sex is ruining one's life.

No matter what the yuffie's sexual preference may be, all yuffies have one thing in common. Yuffies all want to be Woody Allen in bed. And like Woody Allen, they may have performance anxiety on every front—but in bed they are never failures.

PART FIVE

YUFFIES EVERYONE'S HEARD OF

*AT LEAST
EVERY YUFFIE HAS…*

CHAPTER SIXTEEN

THAT RESPONDENT CHORD – THE YUFFIE IN LITERATURE

The yuffie is a popular character in literature—and we include of necessity those forms of literature which come via electronic means or with little balloons drawn over the characters' heads. Every yuffie reads, and every yuffie loves someone to identify with.

Trouble is, until very recently the yuffie was not exactly the *hero* in any literary works. He was the foil, the buffoon: mostly the reprobate whose downfall lay at the moral core of the story. Be a yuffie, hang out with yuffies—God forbid, marry one—and see where it gets you.

Yuffies come in every style in literature—even the late-blooming, weekend, and closet varieties. Fletcher Christian was a late-blooming yuffie—worked himself out of a job and lived out his years on a South Sea island. Babbitt was a yuffie for a few weekends—*he* at least learned he wasn't cut out for the high road, smoking and drinking and carousing, so he took the easy way out. Became an upstanding citizen, of all things.

Closet yuffies abound in literature: living off someone else's money seems to have been a topic worthy of fictionalizing for centuries. Look at Madame Bovary, married to a doctor, no less. It's not her many loves that drive her to distraction: she kills herself over *bills*. No self-loving yuffie would be bothered by such matters. And then there's Nora Helmers, set up in her doll's house by her bank manager husband. Now we don't know what she did when the curtain fell—whether she went out and got a job and became a yuppie, or whether she came back home and quit being a dependent airhead. All we know is that Ibsen didn't like what she was in Act One.

Harry Flashman won every obscure war of the nineteenth century singlehandedly—but then he had a rich wife. Nicholas

---

Secret thoughts of the closet yuffie— in unabashed rhyme:

...I soon got tired of third-class journeys,
  And dinners of bread and water;
So I fell in love with a rich attorney's
  Elderly, ugly daughter.
      Trial by Jury, "The Judge's Song"
      Gilbert and Sullivan

Nickleby wasn't exactly as exciting, to say the least, but think of how much farther he'd have fallen if he hadn't married well-monied Madeline Bray.

Now for the true yuffies in literature. Some lived out lives of penury for love: Elvira Madigan even committed suicide because she couldn't afford to eat. And Alfred Germont was a respectable boy from a nice family until he took up with Camille. Living in the country off the sale of a courtesan's jewels would have made him a closet yuffie, but he started off rich. Besides, he loved her.

Sometimes a fictional yuffie has such a mixed bag of reasons for failure that you figure he exists just so the writer can drive home a half dozen philosophical points around his flawed life. Look at Hamlet: the guy is 30 years old, he has no job, and he's asking his stepfather if he can go back to school at Wittenberg. You can build a first-class tragedy around that.

And Candide. Voltaire didn't write about Candide just for the fun of telling a PG-rated story. No-o-o. There's a philosophical message there. Candide gets into every mess imaginable: autos-da-fe aren't for the light of heart. He flubbed at every turn, couldn't even hack it in El Dorado, which was probably Voltaire's equivalent of the Upper West Side. So what's the moral? Cultivate that garden. Get a job. Candide's no better off than Murray Burns was when he got on the bus carrying his briefcase (see Chapter Twelve).

On the up side, e.e. cummings took a failed life and made a rare exception to the "Posthumous Doesn't Count" law. Born a failure, Uncle Sol failed at everything. Until… "when my Uncle Sol's coffin lurched because/ somebody pressed a button/ (and down went/ my Uncle/ Sol/ and started a worm farm)."*

Attitude and too-smarts account for most true yuffies in literature. Holden Caulfield no doubt grew up to be a yuffie—being thrown out of four prep schools is no mean feat for even the finest yuffie-to-be. (Of course, they could have messed his head around in that hospital: Holden Caulfield now could be approaching retirement from the presidency of a Fortune 500 corporation.)

Bartleby the Scrivener was another one with a bad attitude—you can tell what mood Melville was in at the time. Work? "I

---

*From "nobody loses all the time"—a point we'd argue with you, e.e., if you weren't already *on* the worm farm.

would prefer not to," he said. Maybe it all had to do with having been a clerk in the Dead Letter Office. And what about Miniver Cheevy—born too late. Miniver "scorned the gold he sought"—a true yuffie.

Too smart to be rich—it's surprising there's no previous book on the subject when you see how many fictional characters were too smart to be rich. *La Boheme* is all about starving geniuses—do they burn a manuscript or a chair for heat? Paris was a terrific place to be a yuffie.

Remember George of Albee's Martha and George, immortalized on screen by Richard Burton and wife? He was *in* the history department. A flop, Martha said. A fun guy at a cocktail party, but not one you might choose as father of your children.

Ignatius Reilly got his poor, dead yuffie creator the Pulitzer Prize by sitting in his bedroom and writing about the *rota fortuna* on Big Chief tablets and messing his sheet. It's a typical yuffie sensation, to see oneself up against a "confederacy of dunces."

From Binx Bolling to Dr. Tom More, Walker Percy's books are full of yuffies. Even if Binx does pull in $3000 a month—and almost 30 years ago—he's fallen far from his origins. Guess that's what comes of being a life spectator. The contemplative-sophomore warp, remember?

So much for books. Now you can see yuffies on the screen, 19-inch or silver.

The Reverend Jim Ignatowski's a yuffie beyond believing, doping his way from Harvard to hacking in New York. Tom and Barbara Good are yuffies with a touch of dry British irony. *Cheers's* Diane Chambers was a yuffie to the core of her pompous little being. And Beaver Cleaver—we knew how he'd turn out back in 1959.

Yuffie literary quiz:
Were they yuffies or not?

Dmitri Karamazov
Pip
Eugene and Jamie Tyrone
Countess Ellen Olenska
Philip Marlowe

Discuss it over coffee. If you have to look them up, you must have a job or something.

Jack Nicholson played a yuffie in *Five Easy Pieces*. Imagine an oilfield roughneck who listens to Tammy Wynette actually springing from a family of concert pianists. And being one himself. Pretty good, though Tammy Wynette is not exactly your standard yuffie favorite. There are lots of yuffies in movies. "Graduate" Benjamin Braddock could have been a plastics MBA, but he ended up in the back of a town bus, headed toward nothing but the viewer's speculation. All the Deltas in *Animal House* could have been yuffies, if not for those two minutes at the end when we find out that Brother Bluto grew up to be a U.S. Senator. Alex in *The Big Chill* was definitely a yuffie: look how he ended up. And he didn't even get a cameo appearance. Whether Nick of the same flick also was a yuffie is a close call: drug dealing is one of your more lucrative means of earning a living.

And don't forget the comics. Every yuffie reads the comics on the sly—except those who subscribe to *The New York Times* and feel every day that something's missing as they slurp their Alphabits. *Doonesbury's* Mike is the resident yuffie there— though there are quite a few almost-yuffies in Trudeau's cast. *Cathy* does failure to death, even if she does have a job. And Jon Arbuckle is definitely a yuffie: sitting home all day being tormented by a cat who demands that you bake an entire lasagna is not the road to riches. And have you seen the way the guy dresses?

If you made it all the way through this chapter with a real sense of annoyance, we'll tell you why. There are no cartoons. Just like *The New York Times!* You want to read about literature, you read about literature. You're supposed to be brilliant, remember?

CHAPTER SEVENTEEN

POSTHUMOUS DOESN'T COUNT

OR

THE YUFFIE IN HISTORY

The yuffie in history: it sounds like a contradiction in terms. But the ultimate measure of a true yuffie is to live a life of frustrated genius...or avoidance of success...or both— and to die poor. What counts is *living* penniless: who cares if your paintings sell for half a million two centuries after you're dead? What's it worth if they're playing your concerti in the music halls of the world's capitals, when you died in some wretched little apartment from syphilis? And how would you feel if you knew your novel won the Pulitzer Prize more than a decade after you hooked yourself to the exhaust pipe on your car?

The Yuffie Hall of Fame is a stellar collection. In the arts, the sciences—among the explorers of the world and its would-be leaders. Sure, you studied all these guys (and even a woman or two) in some history course somewhere. Just think: they all got up every morning, just like you, looked in the mirror, and mumbled that they'd be better off if they'd studied accounting instead.

Art
The only thing harder than selling a painting is selling a novel. (Particularly in the sixteenth century, when the novel hadn't been invented yet.) Artists have been the failures of society since the beginning of time. You don't think those sensitive souls who painted animals on cave walls got the prime cuts of mastodon, do you?

Look at Michelangelo. He came by yuffiedom honestly, springing from impoverished nobility. But his mistake was always toiling for someone else: popes and Medicis make corporate America look like Walden Pond. The poor guy slept in his clothes—and sent his check to Dad. Michelangelo had the typical yuffie's bad luck of living to almost 90.

Toulouse-Lautrec gave up the life of nobility to paint in poverty. And don't forget Gauguin. That's a standard yuffie ploy: as soon as your stuff starts selling like hotcakes, take off for Tahiti. Having five kids and syphilis didn't help: Gauguin was a master of self-imposed failure. And his friend Van Gogh undid himself through sheer lunacy.

Matisse got cut out of parental support because of the way he painted—a frequent yuffie happenstance. So his wife sold *hats*.

In the Yuffie Hall of Fame hang more artists than in museums and bathroom showers combined.

GRAVE OF FAMOUS
YUFFIE COMPOSER

Music

They make entire movies about the seamy lives of musicians. And we're not even talking about the ones whose inspiration comes from something they drop in Kool Aid or suck up their noses. We're talking about the guys whose music a yuppie will put on black tie to go listen to.

Mozart. He had all the yuffie beginnings—money and genius. So what did he do? He worked by commission. Where's the sense of immortality in that? Mozart's last concert tour was paid for by possessions he pawned, and Mozart was buried in a pauper's grave. A model yuffie.

Bach tried to support 20 kids on a choir director's salary. Tchaikovsky gave up the law to write music. And married even though he was gay. He probably drank cholera-tainted water *on purpose.*

Most other great yuffie composers achieved yuffiehood only through the uncanny luck of dying young. Bizet died at 37, three months after *Carmen* premiered—and long enough before he knew his work would be famous enough for everyone to be singing "don't spit on the floor" to it. Schubert only made it to 31, Mendelssohn to 38. Hanging in to 39 probably wasn't enough for Chopin.

Music is the one field in which yuffies are somewhat rare. The reason: every famous composer was a prodigy who was performing before kings when he was seven. He never had time to seek out failure. So yuffies in music are to be commended for taking the most public form of early genius and tearing their lives down with it.

Literature

Yuffies are popular hereos—or non-heroes—of fiction (see Chapter Sixteen.) And the creators of fiction are also among the true protagonists in the history of yuffiedom. Picture a novel in progress and what do you always see: some terribly withered myopic fellow (notice how the desks in the homes of famous writers always have a sad little pair of thick wire-rims?) sitting in a garret hunched over a sheaf of paper/typewriter trying to grab a cockroach for tonight's supper. No wonder most writers die of alcoholism.

As the best writer in the history of the world according to everyone, James Joyce is also the best of literary yuffies. He started off young—taking swipes at church and country is no way to get through Catholic school. Joyce survived because he had a rich benefactress, but he was no closet yuffie. He was right out there writing stuff no one wanted to publish. And he was spending every nickel he ever got. Joyce refused ever to let his brilliance get in the way of failure.

His literary colleagues are legion. F. Scott Fitzgerald could have bought himself a nice little house with a picket fence and lived happily ever after. But *no*. His entree to yuffiedom was old Zelda, whose ability to spend has only been superseded by that of Imelda Marcos. Oscar Wilde went to prison just because he preferred men—it didn't do much for his career. O. Henry wrote in prison. And Edgar Allan Poe got thrown out of West Point. Bad behavior may enrich the prose, but it doesn't do much for the pocketbook.

Keats abandoned surgery for literature. His tombstone reads, "Here lies one whose name was writ in water." No wonder. Oliver Goldsmith was saved from arrest for debt by the sale of *The Vicar of Wakefield*. Who'd Samuel Johnson have been without Boswell? A largely unsung yuffie. Coleridge lived out his last years mooching off friends' hospitality. Chatterton committed suicide at 17—a precocious yuffie. And Melville—he became an outdoor customs inspector and died in obscurity.

The writing life hasn't done much good for anyone but Norman Mailer. Why are we bothering with this book?

World leaders

It starts in the Bible. The Bible is rife with yuffies: being a priest or a prophet or an apostle has never been the road to riches. You wrap yourself up in a bedsheet and run around trying to scrounge up followers. And for what? Sure, they all got inscribed in the best-selling book of all times, right up there with Dr. Spock. But did they know it? (Well, that's a philosophical question. Let's decide it over coffee sometime.)

Take Moses for instance. He grew up in a palace, and where'd it get him? He wound up trekking around the desert for 40 years and never even got into Canaan. A yuffie life if there ever was one. (Now, of course, religious leadership is no longer a yuffie vocational choice: just get yourself on a cable TV satellite uplink, and the money comes pouring in. Even if your wife's name is Tammy Faye and your sexual proclivities are up for grabs.)

The yuffie life lies at the core of Buddhism, for Buddha himself was the most exquisite yuffie. He gave up the Brahmin life at the palace to sit under the bo tree and wait for enlightenment. Self-denial…self-torture: Nirvana is reached by freedom of desires. A basic yuffie tenet.

Exploring the world was always a good yuffie choice. Someone spots you for a couple of boats, you cruise around for a dozen years, plant a flag or two, annoy the hell out of your crew, and get buried on some island in the middle of an ocean that nobody heard of before you. They'll name straits and islands and cities in Ohio after you, but you'll never know it.

The most logical person ever to have been a yuffie was Karl Marx. He gave up law to study philosophy, got a Ph.D. but couldn't get a job. He spent 30 years writing his book, supporting six kids off Engels's largesse. "From each according to his abilities, to each according to his needs": the beginning of the eminence of yuffie philosophy.

And then, in the Yuffie Hall of Fame stands one lone soul whose yuffiehood is unequalled in world history. The ever-popular Duke of Windsor. He wimped right along through life until he finally found the exit to failure. It takes quite a bit of doing, to get out of being the King of England. We should all live in such penury—but everything's relative.

"The Yuffie Hall of Fame"

Bella Abzug
Diane Arbus
Bruce Babbitt
Johann Sebastian Bach
Bartleby the Scrivener
Aubrey Beardsley
Ludwig von Beethoven
Charlotte Bronte
Albert Brooks
Buddha
Samuel Taylor Coleridge
Confucious
Christopher Columbus
Captain James Cook
Quentin Crisp
Daniel Defoe
Emily Dickinson
Molly Dodd
Fyodor Dostoevsky
Albert Einstein
F. Scott Fitzgerald
Galileo Galilei
Evariste Galois
Gandhi
Paul Gauguin
Stephen Ginsburg
Vincent Van Gogh
George Gordon, Lord Byron
Nathan Hale
Dashiell Hammett
Gary Hart
Patrick Henry
Homer
Samuel Johnson
James Joyce
John Keats
Jack Kerouac
Martin Luther King
D. H. Lawrence
T. E. Lawrence
Ferdinand Magellan
Mary, Queen of Scots

Karl Marx
Henri Matisse
Carson McCullers
Herman Melville
Michelangelo
Moses
Wolfgang Amadeus Mozart
Edmund Muskie
Richard Nixon
Dorothy Parker
Walker Percy
Sylvia Plath
Edgar Allan Poe
William Sydney Porter
Freddy Prinz
Prometheus
Marcel Proust
St. Paul
Nicholas and
    Alexandra Romanoff
Erno Rubik
George Sand
Sappho
Albert Schweitzer
Percy Bysshe Shelley
Stevie Smith
Socrates
Alfred Stieglitz
Adlai Stevenson
August Strindberg
Piotr Ilich Tchaikovsky
Henry David Thoreau
Alice B. Toklas
John Kennedy Toole
Henri de Toulouse-Lautrec
Antonio Vivaldi
Walt Whitman
Oscar Wilde
The Duke of Windsor
Thomas Wolfe
Virginia Woolf
Zorro

CHAPTER EIGHTEEN

SO, ARE YOU A YUFFIE OR NOT?

Are you a yuffie? Probably: why else did you buy this book? (Or check it out of the library?) (Or find it stuffed in your mailbox in a plain brown wrapper with no return address?)

But, as we've said, sometimes there are fine lines between yuffies and yuppies. Face it, yuffies and yuppies are probably always in the throes of an identity crisis. The yuppie is scrambling up by his fingernails, ever fearful that he'll slip over that line into the murky recesses of failure. And the life of the yuffie is no easy row to avoid plowing: in his dreams of fame, the yuffie runs the constant risk of ballooning up toward fortune.

So take this simple little quiz. Afterwards you can go out and celebrate with a cup of dark roast. Or a nice little glass of chablis. Depending.

QUIZ

1. The bumper sticker on your car reads
   a. "Don't laugh, it's paid for"
   b. "The one who dies with the most toys wins"
2. When your clothes get dirty, you
   a. Wait until Saturday and cart them off to the laundromat
   b. Have the housekeeper stuff them into your Maytag
3. For important papers, you write on
   a. An Olivetti manual portable
   b. An IBM-compatible computer with word processing software and letter-quality printer
4. Your means of transportation is
   a. A Japanese car without the letter Z in its name
   b. A Volvo station wagon
5. You cook with
   a. One saucepan, a pizza pan, and the skillet your mother had when she got married
   b. French enamel cookware
6. For school projects, your fourth grader uses
   a. The library
   b. A new, complete set of the *Encyclopaedia Britannica*
7. Your fourth grader makes
   a. All As
   b. All Cs

8. Your living room wall is covered with
   a. Black and white photos you took in grad school
   b. Abstracts selected by your decorator
9. To plan your old age, you
   a. Pay social security and wait for your inheritance
   b. Invest in gold coins
10. When you feel a strange ache or pain, you
    a. Read the *Merck Manual* until you are paralyzed with fear
    b. Go to a chiropractor
11. To experiment with new experiences for your palate, you
    a. Eat free cheese samples at the supermarket
    b. Go to wine-tasting parties
12. Your history with the phone company is
    a. Fifteen different phone numbers in four states since you left college
    b. The same phone number for ten years
13. The first part of the newspaper you read is
    a. The obituaries
    b. The social columns
14. Your favorite television watching is
    a. Reruns of *"The Honeymooners"*
    b. *"Lifestyles of the Rich and Famous"*
15. Your major literary expenses are:
    a. library fines
    b. Book-of-the-Month Club bills
16. In the 1984 presidential election, you voted for
    a. No one—you're waiting for Eugene McCarthy to stage a comeback
    b. Ronald Reagan
17. To keep track of time, you use
    a. Your instincts
    b. A Rolex
18. Every week without fail, you read
    a. *The New York Review of Books*
    b. *Newsweek*

19. The kind of houseplant you have most success with is
    a. Avocado pits
    b. Scheffleras
20. When you're traveling by foot you wear
    a. Tire-soled huaraches
    b. Reeboks
21. If you have pesky little animals running around your house, they're usually
    a. Cockroaches
    b. Yorkshire terriers
22. When you get up in the morning, you feel like
    a. Having a cup of Ovaltine and going back to bed
    b. Putting on sweats and getting on the Lifecycle

Scoring key: If you psyched out our scoring system by the time you reached question three, you're smart enough to be a yuffie. If you were tenacious and did the whole test, you're driven enough to be a yuppie. So you choose: we're going out for a beer.

GLOSSARY

actuarial tables *n.* longevity statistics skewed by the fact that yuffies live longer than they rightfully should (and never buy life insurance).

aperture flywheeled graumus *n.* typical product of industry; to date its use is undiscovered by Wharton, Harvard, and Bullwinkle.

Calvinism *n.* a pre-destination toward total lack of interest in designer clothing; today associated exclusively with the born-to-fail yuffie. Now completely unrelated to the Protestant work ethic.

capitalistic society *n.* big-bucks-count society. Not to be confused with super-yuffie Marx's *Das Kapital.*

chronic help-refusing complainer syndrome *n.* clinical term for yuffie in therapy. *syn.:* contemplative-sophomore warp fixation.

clipping coupons *n.* activity of the post-inheritance yuffie. Associated with banks, not with supermarkets.

clock-puncher *n.* aggressively employed person.

contemplative-sophomore warp *n.* not to be confused with Vonnegut's *chronosynclastic infundibulum.* In warp one remains age nineteen and hypersensitive for life; time continues to exist.

convenience store *n.* emporium where yuffie can (happily) purchase 1000 mg. of cholesterol, 5000 mg. of sodium, and 50 grams of sugar in two minutes at 300 percent markup.

Cracker Jacks *n.* yuffie's main source of fiber and protein. Preferred caramel popcorn brand because of 1. prize and 2. appearance in *A Thousand Clowns.*

dadaism *n.* nihilistic approach to reality, usually adopted by the yuffie around age six months.

expenditure of energy *n.* 1. yuppie measure of life meaning, similarly, expenditure of money. 2. yuffie measure of life meaninglessness.

failure *n.* the eminently sane process of avoiding prosperity. *obs.:* condition of being insufficient or lacking.

fatalism *n.* the basic doctrine underlying the yuffie's shoulder-shrugging approach to life.

free will *n.* a philosophical phenomenon which, if it exists, connotes responsibility. Generally denied by yuffies (see **Calvinism**).

frustrated genius *n.* synonym for yuffie from 1980 to 1987 (from election of Ronald Reagan to the publication of *Too Smart to Be Rich*).

Godel Escher Bach *n.* the only place where math, art, and music have a harmonious commonality, except on a young yuffie's D-laden report card.

halcyon *adj.* prosperous: usually refers to time in yuffie's past.

jejune *adj.* refers to sounds made when one has too much spit in one's mouth.

Madison Avenue *n.* the avenue between Fifth and Park where yuffies were conceived—and have been summarily ignored ever since.

oppressive *adj.* refers to any person or experience which makes breathing difficult. For the yuffie, usually relates to money.

peon *n.* a lowly drudge: what a yuffie strives never to be, and always ends up being.

philistine *n. syn.:* yuppie.

phlegmatic *adj.* refers to attitude of one who does not clear his throat very often.

polymorphous perversity *n.* a much more acceptable sensation than it sounds.

posthumous *adj.* from Latin *post*—after, *humilis*—humble, usually refers to the time following artistic yuffie's ignominious death.

psychosomatic *adj.* term usually applied when yuppie doctor slept through presentation of yuffie's symptomatology in med school. Such illness usually associated with dominance of creative mind over compliant body.

sexual tension *n.* what makes a yuffie bed vibrate, without dropping a quarter in the box.

social inferior *n.* status of yuffie to yuppie. *syn.*: intellectual superior.

squalor *n.* an experience a yuffie does not have to read Salinger (or Erskine Caldwell, either) to understand fully.

suicide *n.* generally not the way out for the yuffie (see Dorothy Parker's "Resume": "You might as well live.") The Yuffie Hall of Fame is full of exceptions. All were *writers*.

Tao of Physics *n.* treatise in which a yuffie can learn to sit on a beach, staring toward oblivion, and find it all makes scientific sense.

team sports *n.* cooperative effort toward a quantitative goal. A striving for game points in youth usually leads to a yearning for rising stock market points in adulthood. Eschewed by yuffies.

third-world brethren *n.* frequent recipients of yuffies' largesse in the Sixties. Yuffies' financial equals by sheer chance of geography and melanin.

visionary *n.* one who prophesies trends which will be good for someone else. Generally limited to Old Testament prophets, Aztecs, and yuffies living in major metropolitan areas.

"Wheel of Fortune" *n.* not be be confused with *rota fortuna*. Please.